MEETING BIBLE CHARACTERS

ISBN 0-687-09394-5

01 02 03 04 05 06 07 08 09 10—10 9 8 7 6 5 4 3 2 1

Abingdon Press • Nashville

A Holy Mountain

God spoke to Moses from a burning bush on Mt. Horeb. According to Exodus 3:12, God told Moses that the Israelites would worship God at this same mountain. Read Exodus 19:1-6 and complete the puzzle. The letters in the colored box will reveal another name for Mt. Horeb.

Some months after the Israelites escaped from Egypt, they camped in the 1. ____________ in front of a 2. ____________. God told Moses to remind the Israelites that God had helped the people escape, had carried them on eagles' 3. ____________, and had brought them safely to God. The Israelites were to obey God and keep God's 4. ____________ so that they would be a holy 5. ____________.

Scroll of

When God freed the Israelites from slavery in Egypt, God had plans for the Israelites. God's plans included some rules that would help the Israelites serve God. Read Exodus 20:1-8, then

Rules

write the laws on the scroll. (Tip: The Israelites were Hebrews. The Hebrew language is read from right to left. Write the four laws from right to left. Write each word vertically.)

PROTECTION for a *Baby*

Read Exodus 1:22–2:10. Complete the crossword puzzle by remembering what you read from the Bible. If you get stumped, read the Bible passage again. If you successfully solve the puzzle, the letters in the colored boxes (when read from left to right) will spell the name of the baby who was protected.

"Every boy that is born to the Hebrews, you shall drown in the Nile River," 1.______________ told his people. A Hebrew Levite 2.___________ gave birth to a son. For three 3._____________ she hid the baby from Pharaoh and his people. Hoping to save the baby's life, the mother waterproofed a 4.____________, placed the baby inside, and hid the basket among the reeds at the bank of the river. The baby's 5.____________ stood watch nearby. When Pharaoh's 6.________________ came to the river to bathe, she saw the basket and told her maid to bring the basket to her. She discovered a crying baby inside. Filled with compassion, she said, "This must be one of the Hebrew children." Quickly the baby's sister offered to bring a Hebrew 7.___________ to care for the child. Then she brought the child's own 8._____________.

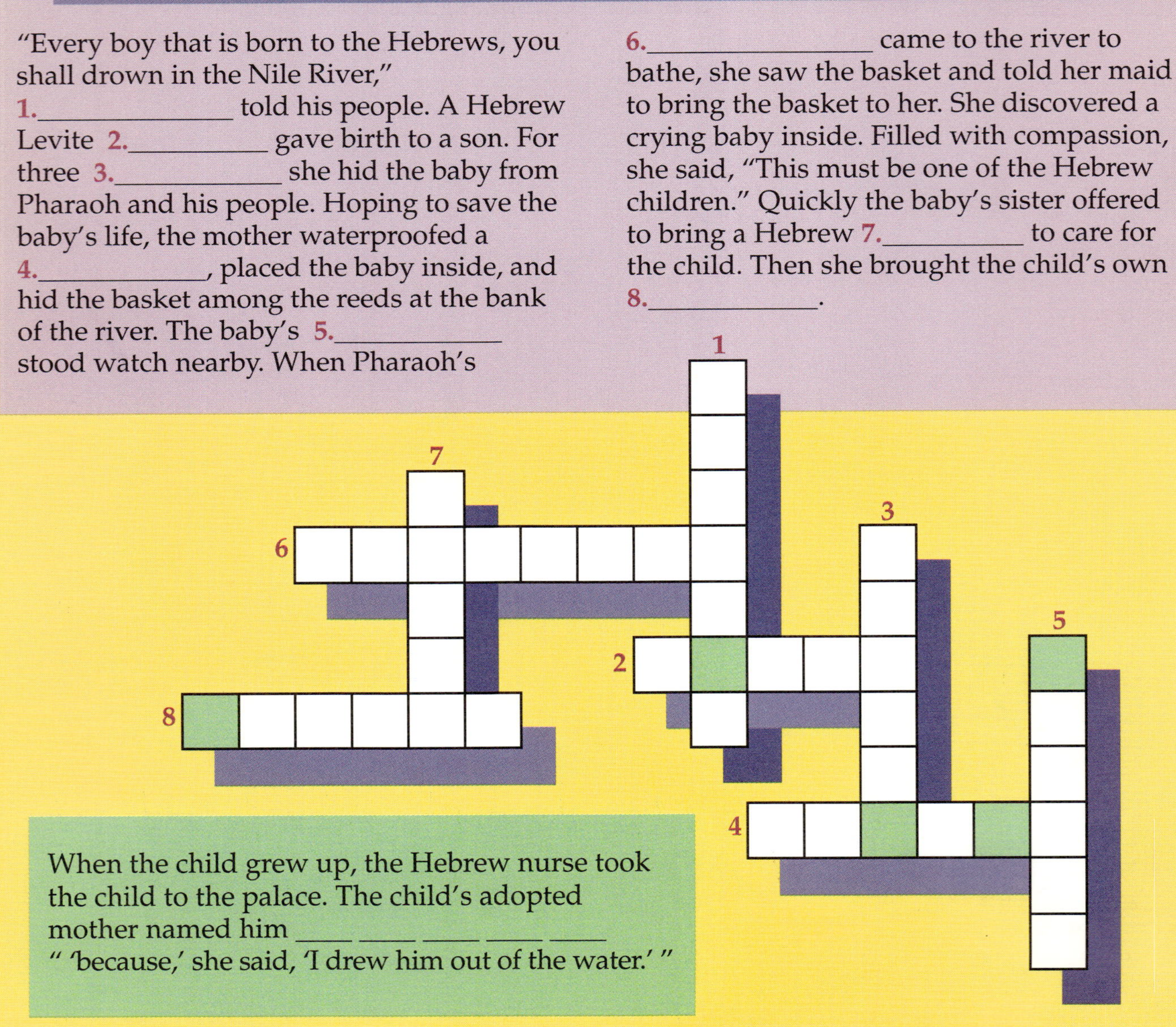

When the child grew up, the Hebrew nurse took the child to the palace. The child's adopted mother named him ____ ____ ____ ____ ____ " 'because,' she said, 'I drew him out of the water.' "

Word Search

Read Judges 6:1-32. Find and circle in the puzzle the hidden words listed below. When you have found all the hidden words, write the remaining letters in order on the blank lines to learn the key verse. Hint: Some hidden words are diagonal; some are backwards!

Midian	Manasseh	Amalekites	camels
Israel	oak	wine press	deliver
Gideon	Egypt	altar	warrior
Baal	hiding	encamp	offering

M	I	D	I	A	N	I	B	A	A	L
A	M	T	H	E	L	L	O	R	D	E
Y	M	O	U	R	G	T	O	D	G	A
Y	A	O	S	L	E	M	A	C	I	R
O	N	W	A	R	R	I	O	R	D	S
F	A	H	I	D	I	N	G	D	E	I
F	S	U	S	N	H	A	L	E	O	E
E	S	L	N	O	E	T	P	L	N	N
R	E	A	Y	R	T	P	E	I	V	C
I	H	E	R	E	P	N	R	V	C	A
N	E	T	O	T	Y	O	H	E	E	M
G	G	O	D	S	G	A	O	R	S	P
F	A	M	A	L	E	K	I	T	E	S
T	H	E	A	M	O	R	I	T	E	S

The Key Verse: ______________________________

____

Amazing Jonah

The words to the story twist through the puzzle below to form a story maze. Put your pencil point on the beginning G, then wind your way through the story, drawing a line through each letter of each word as you go. All the letters in the puzzle should have a line through them when you are finished. Hints: You should not have to lift your pencil point from the paper. Your line should be one continuous line. Some words will turn corners.

Words in the puzzle in order: **God called Jonah. Jonah ran away. Jonah is swallowed by a big fish. Jonah preached God's message. And Nineveh repents. God forgave Nineveh.**

In →

G	O	D	C	A	O	N	A	H	R
S	S	I	H	L	J	H	A	N	A
W	D	B	A	L	E	D	J	O	N
A	E	Y	N	O	J	Y	A	W	A
L	W	A	S	S	A	G	E	A	N
L	O	B	E	V	E	N	I	N	D
F	G	I	M	E	H	R	E	P	E
I	D	G	S	D	O	G	S	T	N
S	E	O	D	F	O	R	G	A	V
H	H	C	A	E	R	N	I	N	E
J	O	N	A	H	P	E	V	E	H

→ Out

Decode a Verse

In a difficult situation, Queen Esther and her relative Mordecai were able to save the life of the king. Decode the Bible verse below to find out more about finding good things in difficult situations.

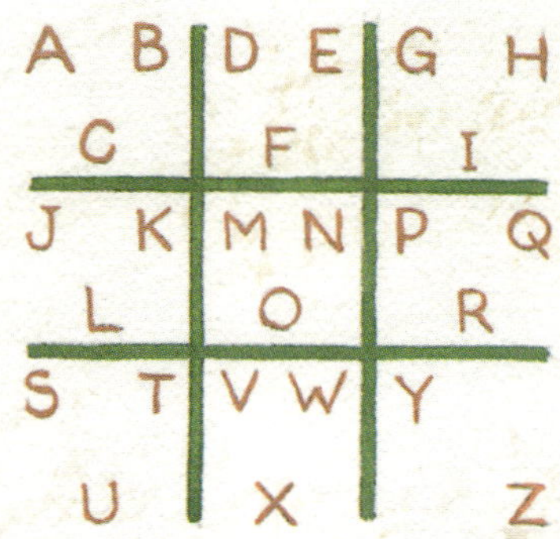

Prophet Search

Throughout history God has chosen persons to help with God's work. Early stories in our Bible tell how descendants of Abraham and Sarah obeyed God. Later God called Moses to lead the Israelites out of slavery in Egypt. When the Israelites reached the Promised Land of Canaan, God used judges and kings as leaders. **Under the rule of some kings, the Israelites failed to live by God's laws. Then God chose persons known as** prophets to proclaim God's message. Use the clues below to help you name eight Old Testament prophets.

Write each prophet's name in the appropriate blank. Then, on another sheet of paper, make your own crossword puzzle by figuring out how the letters in the prophets' names can overlap.

1. First Kings 18:1 ______________________
2. A shepherd from Tekoa became the prophet who called for justice and righteousness. The thirtieth book of the Bible is named for him. ______________________
3. This prophet proclaimed God's love and forgiveness. The twenty-eighth book of the Bible bears his name. ______________________
4. This prophet said that God would teach people to live in peace. The thirty-third book of the Bible bears this prophet's name. ______________________
5. This prophet said that God's law would be written on the hearts of the people. The twenty-fourth book of the Bible is named for him. ______________________
6. Second Kings 2:15 ______________________
7. This prophet told King Ahaz to trust God. The twenty-third book of the Bible is named for this prophet. ______________________
8. Second Kings 22:11-14 ______________________

Micah's Poem

Micah spoke out for God, telling the people that if they did not learn to live with justice and kindness, disaster would come. God also gave Micah a message of hope, so Micah composed a poem. Read Micah's poem in Micah 4:1-4, then complete the sentences below.

1. God will ________________ the people God's ways.
2. When the nations cannot agree, God will ____________ their disputes.
3. Nations will beat their swords into __________________.
4. People will hammer their __________________ into pruning hooks.
5. People will not learn _____________ any more.

Use the answers above to fill in the blanks below. Write the words in order (1-5).

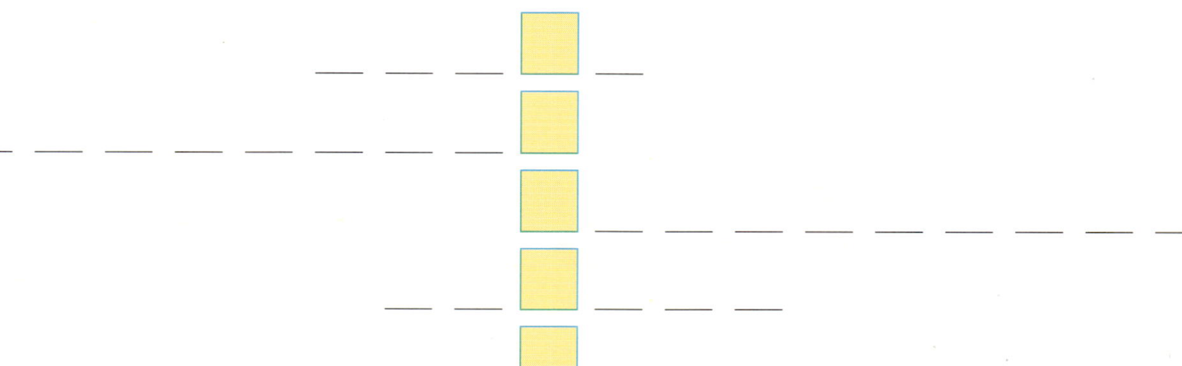

Unscramble the boxed letters and you will learn that Micah's poem was about

_____ _____ _____ _____ _____

God's Message

(1) ___ ___ ___ ___ ___ ___ ___ ___ ___ ___ ___ ___

(2) ___ ___ ___ ___ ___ ___ ___

(3) ___ ___ ___ ___ ___

(4) ___ ___ ___ ___ ___ ___ ___

(5) ___ ___ ___ ___ ___

(6) ___ ___ ___ ___ ___ ___ ___ ___

(7) ___ ___ ___ ___ ___ ___

(8) ___ ___ ___ ___ ___ ___ ___

(9) ___ ___ ___ ___ ___ ___

(10) ___ ___ ___ ___ ___ ___ ___ ___ ___

(11) ___ ___ ___ ___ ___

(12) ___ ___ ___ ___

(13) ___ ___ ___ ___

(14) ___ ___ ___ ___ ___ ___ ___ ___ ___

Use the Bible clues to fill in the blanks. Then write your answers in the puzzle and read God's message from the shaded letters.

Jeremiah 1:1-7

The word of the LORD came to Jeremiah saying, "Before you were born I (1)______________ you. I appointed you a (2)______________ to the nations. Do not say, 'I am only a boy'; for you shall go to all to whom I send you, and you shall (3)____________ whatever I (4)______________ you." God's messages to Jeremiah began in the thirteenth year of King Josiah's (5) ______________.

Jeremiah 1:14; 7:5-9

God said (6) ____________ would break out on all the inhabitants of Judah unless they began to act (7)______________ with one another. They should not (8)____________ the alien, the orphan, and the widow; they should not steal, (9)______________, or make (10)______________ to other gods.

If they began to do as God required, God said, "Then I will (11) ______________ with you in the (12) ______________ that I gave of old to (13) ________ (14) __________ forever and ever."

Word Search

Read Matthew 1:18-24 in your Bible. Hidden in the word search below are fifteen important words found in this passage. How many can you find?

```
D R E A M H A M T W E S S O N
A P I R O L R I G H T E O U S
V C M E S S I A H N U M T A W
I S A P P E R C I D M O B F U
D A R G R E H G Y I K L A J O
U J Y C O D S A N G E L R O F
C E N S P A K P E Q U I W S U
H S O L H T L E M M A N U E L
I U R A E R W C U S R A T P F
L S E R T I V O W L T U Y H I
D A H O L Y S P I R I T E W L
I E N G A G E D H O L U C T L
```

Christmas CROSSWORD

Try to complete the crossword puzzle by recalling the Christmas story.

Down

1. The city of David
2. The first ones to hear the news about Jesus' birth
3. God's messengers
4. An animal feeding trough
5. The shepherds found him lying in a manger.

Across

1. The mother of John
2. An angel visited him in the Temple.
3. The home of Joseph
4. The mother of Jesus
5. Many angels

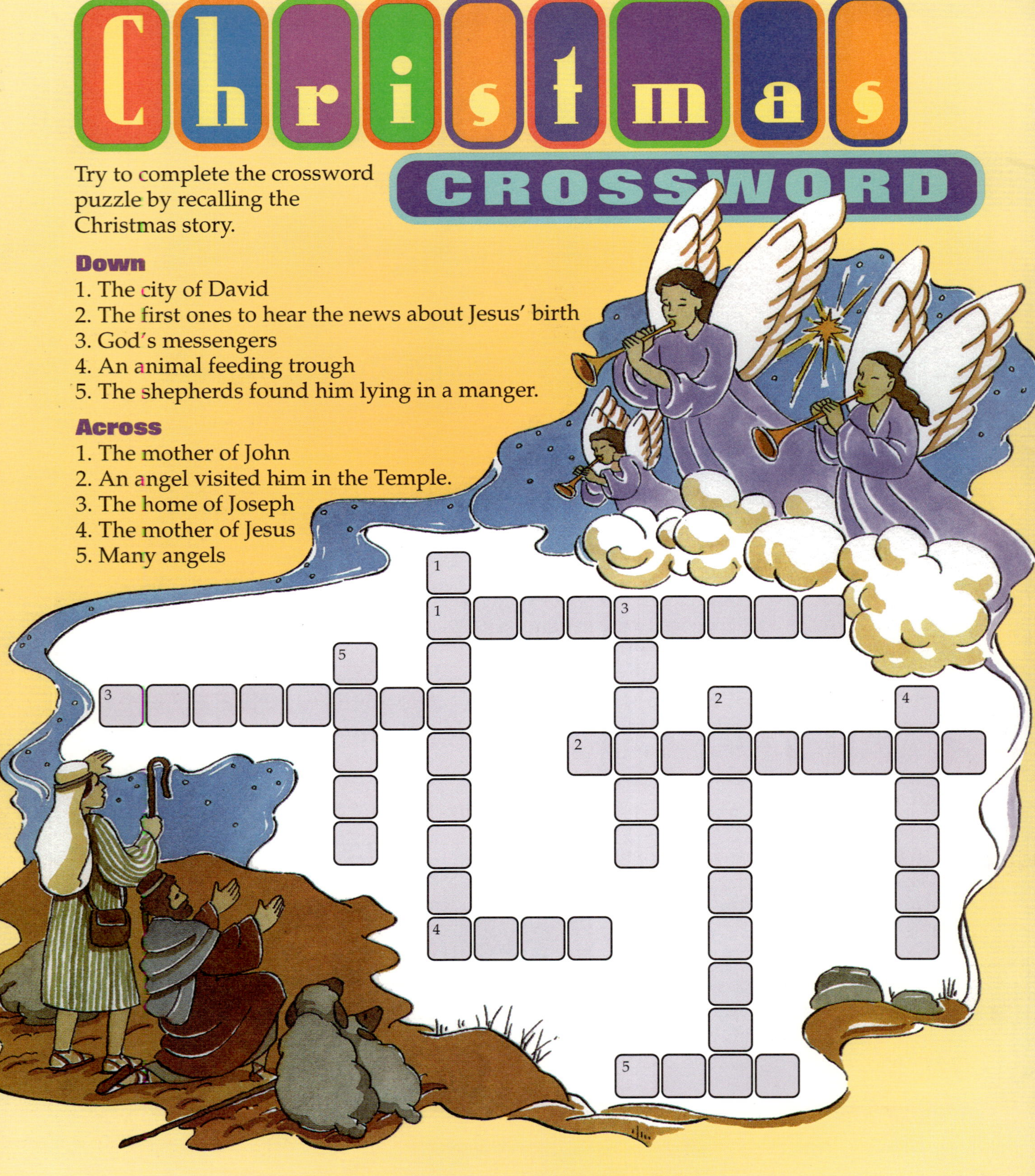

Bible Journey SCRAMBLE

Unscramble the words to complete this story. Check your answers by reading Matthew 2:1-12.

In the time of King **REHDO**, after Jesus was born in **BEEEMHHTL** of **UEAJD**, **SIWE** men from the East came to **URESJLAME**, asking, "Where is the child who has been born **INKG** of the Jews? For we observed his **TSAR** at its rising, and have come to pay him **EGAMOH**." When King Herod heard this, he was **THGIRFDENE**, and all Jerusalem with him; and calling together all the chief priests and scribes of the people, he inquired of them where the **SSIAEHM** was to be born. They told him, "In Bethlehem of Judea; for so it has been written by the **PPTHROE**."

Then Herod **YLTERCES** called for the wise men and learned from them the exact time when the **RAST** had appeared. Then he sent them to Bethlehem, saying, "Go and search diligently for the **LICHD**; and when you have found **MIH**, bring me word so that I may also go and pay him **AGEMOH**." When they had heard the **NGIK**, they set out; and there, ahead of them, went the **TRSA** that they had seen at its rising, until it stopped over the place where the **HCLID** was. When they saw that the star had stopped, they were overwhelmed with **OJY**. On entering the house, they saw the child with **YMAR** his mother; and they knelt down and paid him **OHAMEG**. Then, opening their treasure chests, they offered him gifts of **OLGD**, **KINNARFESNEC**, and **RYRHM**. And having been warned in a **EARDM** not to return to **RODEH**, they left for their own country by another road.

Cast Your NET

ACROSS

1. "__________ me and I will make you fish for people." (Mark 1:17)
2. He was a tax collector. (Mark 2:14)
3. He was walking by the sea. (Mark 1:16)
4. To throw (Mark 1:16)
5. The father of James and John (Mark 1:19)
6. Jesus gave the disciples power to cast this out. (Mark 3:15)
7. Number appointed (Mark 3:14)
9. Brother of Simon (Mark 1:16)
14. "Follow __________." (Mark 1:17)

Down

1. Occupation of Peter and Andrew (Mark 1:16)
8. James and John were _____________ their nets. (Mark 1:19)
10. Observed (Mark 1:19)
11. Nickname for James and John (Mark 3:17)
12. Sea of __________ (Mark 1:16)
13. They were mending their __________. (Mark 1:19)
15. Also called Simon (Mark 3:16)
16. Without hesitation (Mark 1:20)

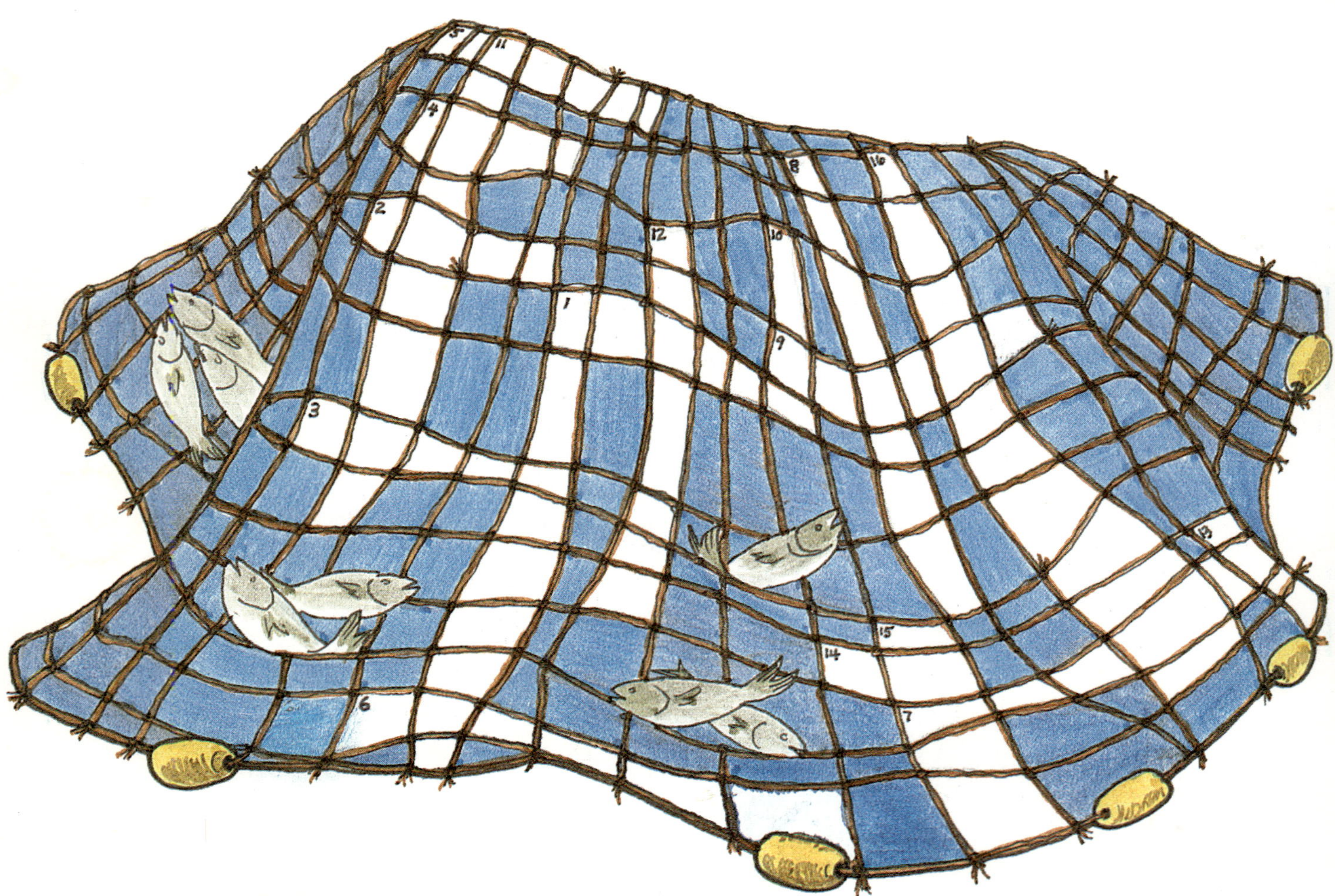

Jesus had many followers. He chose twelve people to travel with him and to teach others. They were called apostles. See if you can find all twelve in this word search. If you need help remembering their names, read Mark 3:13-19.

Find the APOSTLES

```
A J I R B E H O C P A M N S
L A S U T W F D U J T G E O
W M O Y L I M O P E T E R E
S E N T L P A H A M S F Y R
L S I M O N T O G W B C I T
U S J E M A T H O M A S H M
T O U L A R H E N I P D O T
E N D S A G E R F W J A M H
W O A L J U W H O N A J R A
O F S M O B T C H E M G I D
H A I S H R A N D R E W U D
A L S T N F D O H I S O W A
O P C R I N J A M N Q U E E
W H A P A C E L I F T O S U
B A R T H O L O M E W G Y S
K E I L A M W H U B J E D I
M U O S T Q U O P H I L I P
E S T I L O H W R Y C A L E
```

Use your Bible to fill in the blanks with the proper examples. Find and circle those same examples in the word search. They may be horizontal, vertical, or diagonal. Or, look for names of people and places in the word search first, then see if you can guess which blank they fit into. Check your answers in the Bible.

Throughout history, countless people have been killed or martyred for their faith—for example, ________________. (Acts 7:59-60)

There were, in the early church, prophets who acted as God's spokespersons and teachers who helped nurture new Christians in the faith—for example, ________________, ________________, ________________, ________________, and ________________, who was also called Paul. (Acts 13:1)

Missionaries are not always warmly received everywhere they go. Paul and Barnabas found this true in several cities—for example ________________ and ________________. (Acts 13:14, 50; 14:1-2)

Paul was sent by God to take the light of God's salvation to many people—for example, the ________________. (Acts 13:47)

H	I	A	N	D	L	O	I	S	T
B	A	R	N	A	B	A	S	I	L
A	N	T	I	P	A	S	T	M	L
S	T	E	P	H	E	N	U	E	U
E	I	I	T	S	A	U	L	O	C
U	O	T	M	A	N	A	E	N	I
N	C	I	C	O	N	I	U	M	U
I	H	G	E	N	T	I	L	E	S
C	O	N	S	A	T	H	L	A	T
E	G	J	E	S	U	S	Y	N	E

Families where persons claim different faiths are common today. The same was true in Bible times—for example, the family of ________________. (Acts 16:1)

Faith is often passed down from generation to generation—for example, Timothy and his grandmother ________________ and mother ________________. (2 Timothy 1:5)